Living Bread
Reflections for Eucharistic Prayer

Bernard J. Camiré, S.S.S.
Foreword by Cardinal Roger Mahony

BOOKS & MEDIA
BOSTON

ISBN 0-8198-4485-3

Cover design: Helen Rita Lane, FSP

The Scripture quotations contained herein are from the *New Revised Standard Version Bible: Catholic Edition,* copyright © 1996 and 1989 by the Division of Christian Education of the National Council of Churches of Christ in the U.S.A. Used by permission. All rights reserved.

Copyright © 1999, Daughters of St. Paul

Printed and published in the U.S.A. by Pauline Books & Media, 50 Saint Pauls Avenue, Boston, MA 02130-3491.

www.pauline.org

Pauline Books & Media is the publishing house of the Daughters of St. Paul, an international congregation of women religious serving the Church with the communications media.

1 2 3 4 5 6   04 03 02 01 00 99

Contents

Foreword 9

Introduction 11

Our Time Apart with the Eucharistic Christ 13

From the Hands of Jesus 14

Our Bread of Life I 16

Our Bread of Life II 17

Our Bread of Life III 18

Our Bread of Life IV 20

Love's Abiding Presence 21

The Mystery of Divine Love 22

Love without Bounds 23

The Revelation of Love 25

The Proof of Love I 26

The Proof of Love II 27

The Life-Giving Gift I 29

The Life-Giving Gift II 30

The Eucharist Forms the Church 31

The Eucharist Empowers Us 33

The Eucharist, Center of Life I 34

The Eucharist, Center of Life II 36

Sunday Mass and Daily Life 37

The Eucharist: Its Uses, Its Demands 38

The Eucharist:
Proclamation, Liberation, Communion 39

The Eucharist: Our Proclamation I 40

The Eucharist: Our Proclamation II 42

The Eucharist: Our Liberation I 43

The Eucharist: Our Liberation II 45

The Eucharist: Our Communion 46

Our Unworthiness 48

Our Conflicts 49

Our Call to Love I 50

Our Call to Love II 52

Our Call to Love III 53

Celebrating a Fruitful Eucharist 54

Model of Our Mission 55

Heart of Evangelization I 56

Heart of Evangelization II 58

Eucharistic Presence I 59

Eucharistic Presence II 60

Eucharistic Presence III 61

Exploring the Riches of the Eucharist I 62

Exploring the Riches of the Eucharist II 64

Exploring the Riches of the Eucharist III 65

Resurrection I 67

Resurrection II	68
Christ the Lord I	69
Christ the Lord II	70
Christ the Lord III	71
Mary: A Presence Ever Near	73
Appendix	75

Foreword

The Eucharist is central to Roman Catholicism, and truly defines us as a Eucharistic people. From the apostolic age until the present, celebrating the Eucharist "makes the Church." In Word and Sacrament, we express and receive our identity as the Body of Christ through the presence and power of the Holy Spirit. Through this central mystery of the Church, we become a sacrament in and to the world. In accord with both the spirit and the letter of the Second Vatican Council, the Eucharistic Liturgy is the source and summit of the Christian life (*Sacrosanctum Concilium* 10), the heart of our life as God's own people. The other sacraments lead us to the Eucharist, or bring us back to a fuller celebration of this great mystery.

In *The Day on Which We Gather* and *Gather Faithfully Together,* two Pastoral Letters written during my ministry as Archbishop of Los Angeles, I have emphasized the centrality of the Eucharist on Sunday, the Lord's Day. *Living Bread* by Father Bernard J. Camiré, S.S.S., will be a great help to anyone searching for deeper insight into the celebration of the sacrament of the Body and Blood of the Lord. Recognizing the centrality of the regular celebration of the Eucharist, Father Camiré invites us to a deeper appreciation of the practice of Eucharistic Adoration, spending contemplative moments of quiet and repose before the reserved Blessed Sacrament. During such times the heart is moved to gratitude, thanksgiving, petition and praise. Thus, Eucharistic Adoration prepares us for full, conscious, and active participation in the Eucharist, and allows us to continue to taste the fruits after the Mass has ended and we go our ways in peace, love and service.

This collection of brief reflections will enrich our appreciation of the Eucharistic Mystery, especially when read in tandem with the select Scripture passages on the Eucharist which Father Camiré provides in these pages. What is most appealing about this collection is Father Camiré's ability to relate the mystery of the Eucharist and the practice of Eucharistic Adoration to the requirements of charity in our daily lives, and to the demands of justice in a world wider than the Church sanctuary. What's more, these reflections help us to see the Eucharist as the source of strength for healing and reconciliation in a Church increasingly divided, in a world so fragile and broken.

Because the author is impelled by an ardent love for the Eucharistic Lord, his writing does not merely provide information *about* the Eucharist, but awakens in us a felt presence of Christ's real presence in the Eucharist. Father Camiré's judicious mix of reflections, meditations, and select passages from Sacred Scripture makes this volume a welcome and trustworthy companion as we place ourselves in the presence of the Eucharistic Lord.

His Eminence
Cardinal Roger Mahony
Archbishop of Los Angeles

Introduction

"Living Bread and Bread life-bringing"—the sacrament of the Eucharist is thus proclaimed in the incomparable *Lauda Sion,* the sequence for the Mass of Corpus Christi. Here, in poetic conciseness, is a splendid statement about the Eucharist: what it is as the sacrament of Christ's Body, what it is meant to effect in Christ's Church. Such a statement, evocative as it is, does not exhaust the depth of meaning in the Eucharist—nor does any hymn, liturgical text, or passage of Scripture. That is why the theological wealth set before us in the celebration of the liturgy invites us to contemplation—and, in the tradition of the Western Church, to contemplation before the reserved sacrament.

By the grace of God I am called, as a member of the Congregation of the Blessed Sacrament, to daily contemplation before the Eucharist. The years of my priestly ministry have also presented opportunities to share the fruit of my prayer and to write a wide variety of reflections on the Eucharist. At first I contributed to the monthly bulletin of the People's Eucharistic League; in more recent years I have written for the monthly newsletter of the Nocturnal Adoration Society.

Over the years some people who have used these reflections in their personal prayer before the Blessed Sacrament have told me how helpful they have found them in their efforts to reflect on the Eucharist and commune prayerfully with Christ. Their encouragement and favorable comments planted within me the idea of this present collection of meditations.

The contents of this small volume are obviously not a treatise on the Eucharist. I have not followed a strict sequence of thought in considering the sacrament, nor attempted an exhaustive treatment of any of the themes. However, the meditations are arranged to reflect a certain progression of thought. Each meditation, even when part of a particular theme, should be taken up as a distinct entity— to be read, pondered, absorbed and allowed to move the heart to acts of praise, thanksgiving, repentance and petition.

As I pondered again and fine-tuned these reflections, a renewed excitement and appreciation for the Eucharistic mystery stirred within me. I can hope for nothing better than that a like excitement and appreciation may seize the minds and hearts of those who bring these meditations to their quiet time of prayer before the Eucharistic Christ.

Bernard J. Camiré, S.S.S.
Headquarters
Nocturnal Adoration Society
New York City

Our Time Apart with the Eucharistic Christ

"He said to them, 'Come away to a deserted place all by yourselves and rest a while.'... And they went away in the boat to a deserted place by themselves" (Mk 6:31–32). Though the Gospels mention it only infrequently, surely Jesus often invited his disciples to spend time apart with him in quiet repose and intimate conversation. The Master used these special times to provide more detailed instruction and spiritual sustenance for the disciples. The Last Supper climaxed those opportunities when Jesus could open his heart to his intimate friends to reveal the mystery of his person and the depths of his love (see the Gospel of John, chapters 13–17).

Throughout the centuries, the faithful have quite perceptively viewed Eucharistic adoration as an opportunity for present-day disciples to share, in some fashion, the benefits and delights of the original disciples during their times apart with the Master. By means of the Eucharist, the Christ who meets us and communicates himself to us here and now is the Christ who comes as our redeemer.

Jesus' Eucharistic presence, which the Church rightly calls his "Real Presence," speaks of a very personal communication—one that flows from and leads back to our profound communion with Christ when we partake of the Eucharist. This communion with Christ, at Mass and at times of Eucharistic adoration, is that incomparable "moment" when the love of Christ, always one with the love of the Father and the Holy Spirit, yearns to reveal itself to our hearts and encompass our lives.

These times of communion with Christ necessarily bring to mind his sacrificial self-offering, ever rendered to the Father and ever releasing his Holy Spirit upon the world. Jesus invites us to give ourselves as a total gift to him and, with him, to the Father in the Spirit.

The time that we spend with the sacramental Christ in contemplation, if it truly engages our attention and affection, will have a powerful impact on our lives. What Jesus did for his first disciples, he continues to do for us; he inspires, enlightens and nourishes us. As our experience of loving communion with Christ deepens, our sense of charity and unity with our fellow Christians, indeed with all our fellow men and women, is built up and strengthened.

If we dedicate time to prayer before the Eucharistic Christ, we cannot but leave his presence as more enspirited members of his Church—as more effective signs and instruments of his kingdom to the world around us.

From the Hands of Jesus

The Eucharist is Jesus' many-splendored gift to his Church, and in contemplative stillness before the gift, we can savor its splendors. Eucharist-centered reflection stirs a desire within us to know this sacrament in all its richness, moving us to praise exultantly the God who gives with unbounded love. Gradually we come to understand better what it means to live a life nourished on the Bread of Life.

Let us begin by reflecting on the Eucharist in the wonder of its original simplicity—as it was given us from the hands of Jesus. In a Jewish Passover setting, at dusk of the eve before his death, Jesus celebrated a festive banquet with his chosen disciples. The table was set with a variety of food. During this solemn farewell meal, Jesus singled out bread and wine—the food of daily sustenance and the drink of a festive banquet. Jesus took the bread and then a cup of wine into his hands. The blessings he pronounced over them, however, were not the traditional Jewish prayers but the incomparable words: "Take and eat, this is my Body which is given for you.... Drink, all of you; this cup which is poured out for you is the new covenant in my Blood" (cf. Lk 22:19–20).

The Old Covenant of Sinai was sealed in the blood of calves and goats; the New Covenant was sealed in the Blood of Christ. Jesus explained on one occasion: "The bread that I will give for the life of the world is my flesh" (Jn 6:51). He then said at the supper: "This is my Body, given for you." The sacrifice that would take place the next day on Calvary was made present in the celebration of the supper because Jesus himself, given under the signs of bread and wine, was present as victim and priest. In breaking and distributing the Bread "given for you," and in passing the cup "of the New Covenant," Jesus announced his approaching death and set it before the Twelve, and before his Church, as a sacrifice of expiation for the world's salvation.

Jesus added: "Do this in memory of me." The Old Covenant, signifying Israel's deliverance and establishment as God's people, was to be unfailingly commemorated in the Passover celebration. So then Jesus decreed that the New Covenant was to be celebrated unfailingly in the Eucharist as a perpetual memorial of the redemption he effected by his death and resurrection.

Such is the splendid simplicity of the ineffable gift of the Eucharist. May our prayer before the Eucharist release into our minds and hearts the inexhaustible wonders of this gift. May the Eucharist be the center of our spiritual life, and move us to fervent praise and thanksgiving to Jesus for his many-splendored gift.

Our Bread of Life I

In instituting the Eucharist on the night before he died, Jesus did not do something for which his disciples were totally unprepared. He realized that such an awesome and unexpected gift required that he prepare them for it. This preparation took form in the heartening yet challenging words with which he promised to give himself as the Bread of Life. He spoke these words in his famous discourse that followed the miraculous multiplication of loaves by the Sea of Galilee—a miraculous feeding of thousands that highlighted his role as Messiah and also, after a fashion, anticipated the Last Supper.

Despite Jesus' careful preparation of his audience to receive the gift of himself, their minds and hearts failed to grasp his words and intent. He fed the hungry crowd with more than enough bread to stir their faith, but they saw in this miracle only a display of impressive power. Immediately, their minds concocted visions of a mighty national ruler, of restoration of national greatness, and of a new life of prosperity. They focused only on the gift of abundant bread, failing to understand the intention of the giver.

For all our exposure to the faith, are we not at times like the lakeshore audience—eager to receive from God's goodness material, tangible blessings, but slow to hear and live out the full strength of Jesus' teaching? Are we grateful for the blessings of sufficient food and clothing, but somewhat negligent about feeding and clothing the destitute? Do we appreciate the comfort we receive in times of illness and loneliness, while being slow to similarly comfort the sick and desolate among our relatives and friends? Are we delighted to receive the many proofs of Christ's love for us, but reluctant to accept the daily cross of love's demands on us?

Jesus wants to correct our imperfect understanding and to bolster our faltering efforts. That is why—in the mystery of the Incarnation and of the Eucharist—he gives himself so totally as the embodiment of God's Word and presence, of God's truth and grace. May the table of God's Word and the table of the Eucharist continually nourish our life of faith—a life ever sustained in the Son, enlivened by the Spirit, given over to the Father.

Our Bread of Life II

The audience Jesus spoke to by the Sea of Galilee grasped his claims to Messiahship in presenting himself as Son of Man and envoy of God. Then they asked for a decisive sign—something even more wonderful than the multiplication of loaves. Surely the multiplication, to their way of thinking, did not compare with the manna of the Exodus.

Jesus responded that the wondrous gift of the manna was now being fulfilled in the gift that the Father makes of his beloved Son. Jesus is the Bread of Life; his teaching is the real bread from heaven. Manna was a bread from heaven because it descended from above like rain or snow. But in

Jesus, the Father gives an infinitely superior gift, a bread that, in full truth, comes from heaven. The manna that nourished bodies only prefigured the divinely nourishing teaching of the Son of God.

Jesus bore with the spiritual shortsightedness and demands of his audience. He would tell them the full meaning of the gift of himself as the bread from heaven, but he prepared their minds gradually, saying simply that the true bread that gives life is himself as the spokesman of the Father. They need to nourish themselves on his word and his teaching, and the prerequisite for such vital food is to come to him and live in intimate company with him.

As we consider the dialogue between Jesus and his audience, we can reflect that it is entirely God's gift of faith that draws us to the person of Jesus and enables us to acclaim him as God's Anointed and God's very Son. Faith excludes all demands for signs and proofs. May our life of faith be ever such—ever eager to welcome and assimilate into the depths of our being him who, in the word he communicates and the sacrament he bestows, is our Bread of Life.

Our Bread of Life III

Step by step, Jesus has been preparing his audience to believe and receive the full reality of his gift of the Bread of Life. Jesus began by proposing that his words and teachings can nourish the human spirit. Then he set before them the heart of his discourse on the Bread of Life, and uttered the truly startling words: "The bread that I will give for the life of the world is my flesh" (Jn 6:51). With intentional clarity, Jesus was telling his hearers nothing less than that his very flesh is to be their food. Till then, Jesus had said simply that he, the one who reveals the Father's truth, is the bread giving life to all who nourish themselves on it and appropriate it by faith. Then he unfolded the fullness of his message; he spoke of this bread as his very self and of the feeding upon him as eating his flesh.

Whereas Jesus' hearers murmured at his claim that he had come from heaven, they also began to dispute the meaning and credibility of his words: "How can this man give us his flesh to eat?" (Jn 6:52). But Jesus did not change what he had said; rather, he reasserted it and also added a reference to his blood: "Unless you eat the flesh of the Son of Man and drink his blood, you have no life in you" (Jn 6:53). The full realism of Jesus' words then broke in on their minds. For many the effect was shattering, and they would soon turn their backs on him.

The stunning realism of Jesus' words does not trouble us, who regularly eat his sacramental Body in faith; most of us have done so since we were children. We believe the Church's teaching that the Eucharist is truly the Body and Blood of Jesus. But perhaps we have not been as ready to believe what the Eucharist is meant to achieve in our lives. Perhaps we have been slow to grasp that our communion with Christ is a sign and pledge of our resolve to let his charity and peace radiate to persons of all faiths, nationalities and races. May our eating in faith at the sacramental banquet of Christ's Body and Blood so fashion our lives now in his likeness that we shall be readily welcomed to eat at the banquet of never-ending life.

Our Bread of Life IV

Jesus' discourse on the Bread of Life neared its end, and with clear, effective words he revealed the full splendor of his teaching. Communicating in the Flesh and Blood of Jesus will not only nourish a life in God's love now; it will also actuate a bodily resurrection in the life to come. To receive the Eucharistic Body and Blood of Christ is to receive the pledge of future resurrection of the body. Sacramentally joined to Christ in love, the Christian's whole person is gathered to Jesus Christ who will fashion it into the likeness of his glorious resurrection.

Whereas Jesus' audience previously murmured at his teaching, now many among them openly exclaimed that such language is intolerable: How can anyone accept it? (cf. Jn 6:60). Jesus simply replied that his return to heaven must be taken as the proof of his coming from heaven and, therefore, of the authority of his teaching. All that he said about the Bread of Life is to be viewed in the light of two facts: his glorious ascension and the gift of the Spirit. These two facts enable a person to receive Jesus' momentous words with a mind illumined by the Holy Spirit: "It is the Spirit that gives life" (Jn 6:63). The person who hears only carnally, who is disposed to judge only according to the evidence of the senses, cannot grasp Jesus' teaching. The flesh (human nature unaided by grace) is of no help (cf. Jn 6:63).

Many of his hearers reacted to Jesus' tremendous discourse on the Bread of Life with hostile disbelief; they turned their backs on him and followed him no more. The scene has been repeated countless times through the centuries as the Church continues to proclaim Christ's teaching in its fullness—a teaching that proves intolerable for some. We are before a mystery—why some can believe and some cannot. Therefore, may our Eucharistic faith be cause for continual praise and thanksgiving; may it be always sustained with the simple conviction of St. Peter's confession: "Lord, to whom can we go? You have the words of eternal life" (Jn 6:68).

Love's Abiding Presence

With repetition, even the most joyous and exhilarating good news can fail to move our hearts and minds. This is especially true of the Good News that our Christian faith unceasingly proclaims to us. From time to time we do well to try to hear with new awareness the revealing message of Jesus' boundless love for us, with all the wonder, joy and life which it entails.

As Christian piety has grasped, this love is revealed preeminently in the Eucharist. As Jesus' ineffable gift of self, the Eucharist satisfies a vital need of his heart; it is the most visible and convincing proof of his tremendous love.

The reserved Eucharist can and should be seen as Jesus' abiding presence of love. Though the celebration of the Eucharist has primary importance, that does not exhaust its significance as a sacrament of love and communion. Christ, reserved in the tabernacle, dwells in our midst, a guest who desires our presence in return, so he can continue our formation in Eucharistic love and life. Our prayerful presence is an effort to return love for love, an effort to discover in the ever open heart of Christ the love, counsel, help and consolation we need.

With strong and enduring love our Savior chooses to

abide with us sacramentally, despite our indifference and neglect. In the silence and mystery of his presence, he awaits our presence in response. Our anxious hearts, wounded spirits and troubled minds need him so much. The abiding Christ of the Eucharist is a fountain of life-giving water which satisfies our spiritual thirst and refreshes us inwardly.

The Mystery of Divine Love

A mystery is at work in the way love, in its varied expressions and intensities, comes to life and changes human hearts in both subtle and dramatic ways. We see the mystery in a rudimentary way in children who find delight and harmony in their friends. We see it in a mature form in a close-knit family living through life's joys and sorrows. We see it in all its power, depth and beauty in a man and woman who bind their lives irrevocably in the marriage covenant.

These examples of human love hint at the mystery of divine love, of the God who is the community of love—Father, Son and Holy Spirit—and who ever seeks to share that intimate community of love with us. Of all the means that God has devised to gather us into the divine community of love, the Eucharist holds first place.

Through the Eucharist, Jesus shares a community of life with the faithful of his Church. Jesus, the Lord of glory, clothes himself in the simple appearance of bread to share something of our humble, fragile condition. He gives himself to us in a meal that we may experience his saving presence which encourages and revitalizes us. According to the thought of St. Peter Julian Eymard, a 19th century apostle of the Eucharist, the sacramental Christ offers us his joy and blessedness: "Who is the faithful Christian who has not, at one time or another, tasted the savor of this true manna from heaven, and was not, at least for a moment, elated with peace and happiness."

The Trinity, the divine community of love, seeks unceasingly to gather us into their company and share with us their peace and blessedness—to share with us, who are human, mortal and imperfect, something of the divine, the eternal, the perfect. May we ever find at the Eucharistic table and at Eucharistic prayer our access to this divine community, and thereby be formed progressively into that community of love which is the body of Christ, the Church.

Love without Bounds

When the Twelve sat down with Jesus to celebrate the Paschal Supper on the night before he died, they could never have imagined the extent of the love he would reveal during that meal. This love would test the faith of Christian disciples in all ages to come, and at the same time would take God's self-gift to us to the very limit.

During the Paschal Supper, Jesus revealed how he would be taken from his disciples through a bloody death on a cross for the world's salvation, and at the same time how he would remain with his disciples—with his followers of every century. At climactic moments within the meal, Jesus uttered altogether extraordinary words over bread and wine: "This is my Body which is given for you. This is my Blood of the new covenant." What still retains the appearance of bread and wine is now, truly and really, the Body and Blood of Jesus Christ. The divine love that removes Jesus from human sight through his salvific death also brings his abiding presence into being.

Jesus then added the command: "Do this in remembrance of me." With these words, Jesus bridged the seemingly impossible: to give his life in total love once for all on cross-crowned Calvary hill, and yet to bestow that same loving gift of self to Christians in every age till the end of time. Divine love spans and embraces the centuries by bringing Calvary's victim to the altars of Christians, of every time and place, gathered to celebrate Mass.

The disciples then heard the most stunning words of all, with which Jesus satisfied our human desire for heart-to-heart union with God. He didn't remove us from our earthly condition, where we cannot yet possess the intimate mutual self-giving between God and us that heaven affords. Yet we can experience the greatest union possible here. As Jesus broke the bread which had become his Body, he said to his disciples, "Take and eat!" As he passed the cup of wine which had become his Blood, he invited them, "Drink of it, all of you!"

Little wonder that the Church, the Bride of Christ, sings enthusiastically on Holy Thursday and throughout the year of her Lord's Eucharistic presence, sacrifice and nourishment. For at the Last Supper God's incarnate love burst upon the world in a love bestowed to the limit of self-giving, in a love outpoured till the close of time, in a love unto the end.

The Revelation of Love

As the summation of Jesus' love of the Father and of humanity, the Eucharist embraces Jesus' whole life which culminated in Calvary's sacrifice, and includes his exultation in the Father's glory. Through the Eucharist, Christ reaches out to us and draws us to himself to experience the saving grace of his life and the bounty of his love. The Eucharistic embrace of Christ constantly enlivens and sustains the Church.

The Church delights daily in this sacramental gift of love's making. Christ reigns with the Father in heaven's realm, yet through the Eucharist he comes to us and remains with us in intensely personal closeness—a closeness that allows the Church to claim that it continues Christ's loving presence and activity in the world.

With one of Scripture's most common and expressive symbols, Jesus spoke of the love-bond between himself and Christians in terms of the vine and the branches (cf. Jn 15:1–9). Intimately joined to Jesus, the members of the Church are like healthy branches joined to the life-giving vine stock. They form but one vine, sustained by the same supernatural sap. When the branches draw unceasingly from the nourishing sap, they yield abundant fruit.

Intimately associated with the metaphor of the vine is the precept of love which must characterize Jesus' disciples (cf. Jn 15:10–13). They cannot form a united, living community unless they remain in the bonds of mutual love. The love which makes possible such enduring and intimate communion is none other than the love which unites Father, Son and Holy Spirit.

This outpouring of love within the Godhead is daily extended to us in the Eucharist. When we fervently partake of the "fruit of the vine" we invite God to let his love course through our being; we invite Christ to fill us with his life and spirit. With the sacramental Christ, the Church becomes love's revelation when it allows the Eucharist to have its full unitive effect in ecclesial life.

The Proof of Love I

To be fully authentic, human self-giving needs to express itself in bodily form. Through the body's activities and energies love goes beyond pious wishes and becomes active in deeds. Love attains its height through the surrender of the body to death for the sake of another: "No one has greater love than this, to lay down one's life for one's friends" (Jn 15:13).

In his relation with us, God chose to respect this truth that governs relations among humans. The Evangelist John declared this truth in the incomparable phrase, "And the Word became flesh and made his dwelling among us" (1:14). If the Word of God is to give himself to us in utter love, he can only really give himself in the form of flesh and blood. What God has to say to us and do for us, he now says and does in bodily terms, with his flesh and blood.

Authentic human love eventually proves itself in bodily deeds. We do something for the person loved; we accept hardship, go out of our way, give up some of our time for the other. But no matter how ardent and selfless, human love bumps against boundaries, both psychological and bodily. No matter how passionate and self-donative human love may become, flesh cannot fuse with flesh. Our human, fleshly existence limits the extent of our communion with another.

Only the Word of God, who became flesh and dwelt among us, can bring about the mystery of being in bodily form and yet going beyond its boundaries. With those daring yet blessed words, "Take, eat; this is my Body. Drink; this is my Blood," Jesus invites us to take his true, real, substantial presence into ourselves. Such is the radicalness of divine love!

As the Son of God transcends the boundaries of flesh to enter into us and embrace us with his love, so does he ask us to break down our boundaries of selfishness and self-will in response to his love. When we gradually move beyond our boundaries through Eucharistic Communion, our being opens out to God and neighbor with the expansive charity of Christ. In his body, the Church, we are partakers of "the fullness of him who fills all in all" (Eph 1:23).

The Proof of Love II

The Christian faith does not teach that God is a Being closed in on himself in cold, solitary uniqueness. Rather, God exists eternally in loving intercommunion: from the very beginning the Word, the Son, is in the bosom of God the Father; he is one with him in the communion of the Holy Spirit. The Trinity, God three persons sharing one nature, is a mutual self-giving intercommunion of persons—a mystery of Being and Life that exceeds all we can imagine. Every human person is called in some way into this mystery of Being and Life.

But is all this too extravagant? Is it just pious talk? It would certainly be no more than that if all we had was human speculation or the mystical musings of individuals. But the basis of what the Christian faith declares of God and of the human vocation in relation to God lies in Jesus Christ—in his life, word, passion, death and resurrection. Jesus proclaimed himself to be the eternal Father's Word communicated to the world. He proved this claim through his complete obedience to the Father and his total self-surrender to the Father for the redemption of the world. Jesus' obedience and self-surrender reveal a divine love for us—a love proved by deeds of flesh and blood.

These deeds became manifest in Jesus' whole life, but especially in the breaking of his body and the pouring out of his blood in his passion and death. These deeds of divine love, in Christ, continue to reach us in our celebration and reception of the Eucharist. They continue to flood our souls and wash away our egoism and resistance to God's will.

Whether we humans will have it so or not, in God we live, move and have our being. But divine love goes beyond this through the Eucharist, wherein the Body of the incarnate Word invades our life, breaks the shackles of our self-centeredness, with its isolation and loneliness, and brings us back into communion with the Triune God. When we at last unreservedly open our lives to the Eucharistic Body of Christ, we recognize, welcome and respond to the fleshly proof of God's love.

The Life-Giving Gift I

"I am the living bread that came down from heaven. Whoever eats of this bread will live forever" (Jn 6:51). Jesus spoke these startling words while contrasting the gift that he will give with the gift that God gave to the children of Israel in the desert, the manna.

Jesus' words about a new gift of "living bread" were a preparation for what he would give in the upper room. So the manna, the bread which came down from heaven, prefigured the mystery of the Eucharist, the gift of Jesus' very self, the gift of Jesus' love which gives life to the community of believers and renews it continually.

The Eucharist is the indispensible nourishment for the new People of God, the Church. As we allow the Eucharist to penetrate our souls, hearts and minds, we are built up into Christ's Mystical Body. As St. Paul expressed it, "Because there is one bread, we who are many are one body, for we all partake of the one bread" (1 Cor 10:17).

The Church and the Eucharist are so intimately related that we can say the Church is reflected in the Eucharist as in the fountain from which its own life springs. If this is true in regard to our experience of unity and charity among ourselves, it is true also in regard to the difficult, demanding, even harsh aspects of Christian daily living. Everything in us is called to participate in the attitude of a willing and unconditional surrender to the will of our heavenly Father.

In each celebration of the Eucharist, the Church returns to its source of life. This is why the Church insists on the weekly celebration of Mass, as a minimum under normal circumstances. The insistence flows from the unequivocal words of Jesus, "Unless you eat the flesh of the Son of Man and drink his blood, you have no life in you. Those who eat my flesh and drink my blood have eternal life, and I will raise them up on the last day" (Jn 6:53–54). The Eucharist is truly Christ's gift of life to his Church.

The Life-Giving Gift II

For Catholics of Western Christendom a highlight of June is the feast of Corpus Christi. With its loving focus on the sacrament of the Eucharist, this feast proclaims a truth that the Catholic Church proposes consistently and boldly: that the Eucharist is really the Body and Blood of Christ. This gift of Jesus' very self is given us that we may have life: "Unless you eat the flesh of the Son of Man and drink his blood, you have no life in you.... Those who eat my flesh and drink my blood abide in me, and I in them" (Jn 6:53, 56). This gift of food is unparalleled in its potential for giving life.

The Church's great theologians and spiritual masters have repeated a truth about this sacramental food, namely, that when we assimilate ordinary food, we change it into our own substance; however, when Christ gives himself to us as Eucharistic food, we are transformed into him. When we give free rein to the effect of this sacramental eating, the words of St. Paul take on their fullest meaning, "It is no longer I who live, but it is Christ who lives in me" (Gal 2:20).

The extent to which the Eucharist can influence and transfigure our lives fills us with wonder and praise, but our understanding of this sacrament would be incomplete if we did not consider its demands. If Christ chooses to fill and act upon our being so intimately, it is so that our minds and hearts may take on something of the boundless dimensions of his mind and heart.

Eating the Eucharistic Body of Christ makes us profoundly aware of the whole body, the Church, that is fed. "Because there is one bread, we who are many are one body, for we all partake of the one bread" (1 Cor 10:17). Eating the Eucharist is not our private devotion, our solitary supper; it is our progressive immersion into that grace of the Holy Spirit which forms the Church, as Christ's body, in unity, charity, truth and peace.

When we are completely receptive to the power of the Eucharist, Christ does with us today what he did with the bread of the Last Supper: he takes us and blesses us; he "breaks" us, and he gives us for the sake of others. Christ gives us to eat of the Eucharist, that we might be eucharists for the life of the world. Like the Eucharistic presence of Christ that consoles, reassures and nourishes, we can be present to our neighbor—whether next door or halfway around the world—who needs to be consoled, reassured and nourished. When the grace of the Eucharist truly fills the energies of our minds and hearts, when it truly fills our capacity for Christ-like love of others, then the Eucharist's potential for giving life is indeed unparalleled.

The Eucharist Forms the Church

When we reflect on the Eucharist as it builds up the Church, we quickly realize that it forms the Church in many ways. Basic to them all, however, is the actual celebration of the Eucharist according to the mind of Christ our Lord.

When the Church celebrates the Eucharist, it praises and adores God, and voices its gratitude for the mystery through which the Church is constituted. The Eucharist embodies and extends to us, in our particular time and place, the redemption Christ Jesus wrought for us. In this mystery of faith we, as people of the Church, learn what it means to be creatures, in relation to God and to all created beings. We learn to embrace lovingly and live responsibly this dimension of our being.

This basic attitude involves an ardent, persistent quest for God above all else; it involves putting his kingdom first in our lives. This sentiment and the stance it entails are not welcomed in our contemporary culture. Therefore, the Church ever needs the Eucharist to bring into being, to restore and renew this sentiment and stance in its people.

The Eucharistic celebration builds up those who are genuinely open to the mystery of God, to adoration, to the meaning of providence, to unselfishness in living out the teaching of Jesus and his Church. The celebration of Mass, even for those who have not studied theology (as the history of the Church shows unmistakably), helps people understand God as the Absolute Mystery of life, to be adored and thanked.

Where this fundamental sentiment toward the divine is absent, human beings act according to secondary absolutes, such as truth, justice, equality and fraternity. But eventually, however noble these absolutes are in themselves, they prove to be inadequate and cause frustration and conflict.

The sentiment and stance by which we relate authentically to God and his creation are brought to life and nurtured in us as people of the Church. Frequently, and even daily, we are invited to immerse ourselves in the celebration of the Eucharist, for it is only in living responsively and fervently from the Eucharist that we are progressively formed into all that Christ expects us to be as his Church.

The Eucharist Empowers Us

What does it mean to say the Eucharist empowers a Christian's life? Drawing from the prophet Isaiah, we can say it means to live in such a way that one's life is directed outward to others, not closed in on itself with a constant yearning for "self-realization" or "to be somebody." It is a life emptied of selfishness.

Such a Eucharistic life devotes itself unstintingly to tasks beyond self. Isaiah sets forth these tasks in the words: "To bring good news to the oppressed, to bind up the brokenhearted, to proclaim liberty to the captives, and release to the prisoners...to comfort all who mourn...to give them a garland instead of ashes, the oil of gladness instead of mourning, the mantle of praise instead of a faint spirit" (Is 61:1–3). These tasks define a life lived for the service, consolation, joy and salvation of others.

What motives generate such a life directed generously beyond itself? St. Paul gets to the heart of this question when he says, "For we do not proclaim ourselves; we proclaim Jesus Christ as Lord and ourselves as your slaves for Jesus' sake" (2 Cor 4:5). In other words, the life of the Christian we are describing here is not taken up with a selfish cause, but with the "cause" of Christ. It is a life free of all worry about personal success or its lack, because any problems met while serving others in the spirit of the Gospel are entrusted to the Lord as his "problems."

Needless to say, a life that is utterly devoted to others for the sake of Christ is constantly inspired, nourished and animated by the living person of Christ. This happens more surely and powerfully in our encounters with the Eucharistic Christ in the liturgy and in prolonged meditative prayer. In the Eucharist Christ embodies and manifests his total sacrificial love for humanity; through the Eucharist Christ draws us into the dynamism of that sacrificial love. He empowers us to break through the shell of self-centeredness and extend ourselves generously in life-giving service of others.

The Eucharist, Center of Life I

In John's Gospel we find Jesus' confident declaration: "I...will draw all people to myself" (Jn 12:32). This statement does not refer directly to the Eucharist, but when heard in context it can help us to grasp the profound meaning of the Eucharist (cf. Jn 12:20–36). This statement sheds light on the interior power of Jesus' saving death and resurrection, which the Eucharist brings to realization and manifests sacramentally.

The Evangelist John tells us that some Greeks who had gone to Jerusalem for the Passover feast desired to see Jesus, for they had taken an interest in him. The vast outreach to the Gentile world that would soon take place was here foreshadowed.

Jesus could have easily drawn these devout Greeks to himself by performing some stunning deed, but his response seems disappointing. They were not shown anything striking; rather, they heard only figurative talk about a grain of wheat falling to the earth and dying (Jn 12:23–24). Jesus was speaking about his death: a death that would definitively reveal the Father's love; a death that would glorify the Son of Man and bring forth new life for the world. Raised on the cross, Jesus would be displayed as the Savior of the world for all to see. He would draw all people to himself to gather them into his personal self-offering in love to the Father.

Jesus' death and resurrection effects universal reconciliation and communion, both between humanity and God, and with people among one another. This means that Jesus' death and resurrection needs to be available to the world in the form of some sign that will reach all persons, attracting them to Jesus and, together with him, drawing them to the Father.

Among its wondrous qualities, this sign will express and bring about the communion of human beings with Christ. It will gather them into and secure them in an assembly of grace, the Church. It will progressively gather them into Christ's sacrificial self-giving to the Father in loving adoration and filial obedience.

This sign of which we are speaking is the Eucharist. This sign fosters union with God, heals wounded souls, assures anxious minds and satisfies imploring hearts, for this sign is nothing less than the sacramental presence of the world's crucified and risen Savior.

The Eucharist, Center of Life II

For Catholic Christianity, the Eucharist is at the very center of the Church's life and activity. The Eucharist is the sacrament that makes of many people a single body, the body of Christ in the Holy Spirit. The Eucharist gradually forms a people through which the Spirit of Christ transforms history and creates a new humanity according to God's designs.

The Eucharist brings about God's kingdom in the world not by human might but by the power of the Spirit of the risen Christ. Therefore, putting the Eucharist at the center of our lives means recognizing the power of this sacrament and allowing it to act in us as individuals and also as a Christian community. It means allowing the redemptive power of Jesus' dying and rising to break through time and transform human history.

This wondrous effect upon our world, achieved through us as the body of Christ, is possible because the Eucharist puts us in living contact with Christ, who is the very center of Church life and of all human history. It does this through its real though mysterious identity with Jesus' paschal sacrifice.

The Eucharist is meant to hold a preeminent and vital place in Christian life, not only by frequent participation in the Mass but also by meditative prayer that focuses on the Eucharist. Our contemplation of the Lord's sacramental Body fosters a more lively awareness that the Eucharist holds the central place in Christian life. It helps us understand the role each of us plays in allowing the power of Christ's saving death and resurrection to reach and transfigure our world according to God's design.

Sunday Mass and Daily Life

For many years now there has been a keen concern within the Church that Catholics understand and live out the close connection between daily life and the celebration of Sunday Mass. The subject is crucial, for if worship is seen as having no bearing nor impact on life, it is bound to be questioned. If the Eucharist is the sacrament of perfect praise, the sacrament *par excellence* of charity, reconciliation and unity, then these realities are to be expressed in daily living.

The action of Jesus by which he gives himself completely to the Father for the salvation of the world and which he himself repeats sacramentally in every celebration of the Eucharist can deeply affect our Christian lives. It can fuel in us an ever greater capacity for self-giving, courage and a commitment to serving our neighbor. Thus it will help us see all of life as a call to unconditional love.

This mystery of love which we celebrate regularly in the Mass is meant to bear daily fruit in our personal lives, and through us create a climate of forgiveness, healing, selflessness, unity and peace within society. This mystery of love not only nurtures in us an ongoing sense of communion with God, it also moves us to take an interest in and to help our neighbor. It calls us to work at changing the structures and situations that gravely threaten or assail the dignity and rights of fellow humans.

Such a view of Sunday Mass is far removed from seeing it only as a duty to fulfill or as the occasion for a welcome spiritual uplift. Instead, the Eucharist is seen as the means whereby Christ takes hold of and transforms all the moments of a Christian's life.

Understanding and living out Sunday Mass in this way does not happen automatically. It springs from prayerful reflection that both precedes and flows from the celebration of Mass. Prolonged silent prayer before the Blessed Sacrament helps us grasp the full meaning of the Eucharistic celebration and experience its urgent call to Christ-like behavior in daily life.

The Eucharist: Its Uses, Its Demands

In Catholic life today, is there a danger that we emphasize the sacrament of the Eucharist for its uses, while we shirk its demands? If such a danger exists, it probably does not crop up in explicit statements, but surfaces in subtle ways.

For example, some might stress that the Eucharist is the sacrament of unity. The Christ who reconciles God and humanity gives himself as the sacramental Bread, which all who confess his name must eat in order to draw from him the grace of reconciliation and unity with fellow men and women. Others might insist that the Eucharist is the sacrament of liberation. The Christ who sacrifices himself even unto death to free all persons from the oppression of sin gives himself sacramentally. Thus, all who believe in him can draw inspiration, courage and strength in their struggle with sin's tyranny in the world.

These truths and values flow from a clear grasp of the Eucharist. Yet one could propound them while failing to understand the Eucharist's core reality, the essential requirement. We could value the Eucharist for its uses in creating a more just, humane, fraternal society, and fail to see what it asks of us personally. When this demand is fulfilled, the sacrament's wider influence will be felt within society. In nourishing us with the Eucharist, Christ asks of us an ever deeper conversion of heart, an ever more generous gift of self that joins us to him in his selfless love of the Father and of humanity.

When we regularly focus our prayer on the Eucharist, we can contemplate the dimensions of this sacrament in all their truth, richness and demands. In prayer, we have a precious occasion for probing the meaning of the Eucharist not simply as a good at our disposal for fashioning the world's well-being but as the living presence of Christ. He enfolds us with the power of the Holy Spirit—a power that draws us ever more deeply into the Son's obedience and openness to the Father's will for the world's salvation.

The Eucharist: Proclamation, Liberation, Communion

Those who, in their time of quiet prayer before the Blessed Sacrament, ponder the meaning of the Eucharist understand that this sacrament is not simply an object of worship unrelated to what happens in our world. Those who pray deeply before the Eucharist know that this sacrament lies at the heart of what Christians are and do in the society about them. The Eucharist makes an important difference for the Christian who takes seriously his or her task of Gospel witness and apostolic outreach—a witness and an outreach that can be summed up in three words: proclamation, liberation, communion. Each of these elements bears an intimate relationship to the Eucharist.

Because it is the sacramental celebration of the Lord's death and resurrection, the Eucharist is the life-giving core of the Church's proclamation of the Good News. Without this sacrament the Church's ability to evangelize effectively would break down. For if the preached word of the Christian Gospel is to bear fruit, it has to be nourished by the sacramental Word, as bread broken and wine poured out for our salvation.

Because the Eucharist gives us access to the act of Christ which saves and heals us, it frees us of all that prevents us from being what we are meant to be as children of God and brothers and sisters in Christ. It spiritually liberates us as we relate to God and our fellow humans.

Finally, authentic Eucharistic proclamation and liberation bring about communion—a communion stamped with the hallmarks of charity, peace and fellowship. Only such communion shows true Christian liberation and proclamation.

It will spiritually benefit us to reflect often on the Eucharist as proclamation of the Gospel, as freeing event, and as experience of communion. All three aspects come into play in our relationship with God and with our fellow men and women. All three aspects are found in the New Testament picture of the apostolic Church; all three need to find full expression in the Church today.

The Eucharist: Our Proclamation I

We read in St. Paul: "For as often as you eat this bread and drink the cup, you proclaim the Lord's death until he comes" (1 Cor 11:26). We have often heard these words, but have we understood their depth of meaning and their implications for Christian life?

We believe that when we celebrate the Eucharist Christ makes his redemptive sacrificial death present to us sacramentally. But do Paul's words contain more than this basic statement of belief concerning the Christian Eucharist? Yes, they do—if we understand that Christ wishes to be vibrantly present and active in all of us who participate in the celebration of the Eucharist. Jesus' death, his sacrificial self-giving to the Father, is proclaimed when we allow him to "be" in us, to act in us. This happens as we live the Gospel's demands and as we reach out to other people with the heart, mind and spirit of Christ. When we allow Christ to be present and active in us in this way, we are "laying down" our lives for love of God and our neighbor; we are extending in our time and place the saving effect of Christ's laying down of his life so many centuries ago.

When we participate in the Mass with this understanding of "the death of the Lord," our Eucharist does not simply proclaim our belief in the presence and power of Christ's sacrament. It also proclaims our readiness and resolve to be the saving Body of Christ (bread "broken," wine "poured out") for the world. Our celebration of the Eucharist declares that as we extend ourselves in selfless service of others we are putting our lives on the line with Christ. We are taking up the cross to follow him; we are accepting a share in the Lord's sacrificial self-giving.

For those who wish to live deeply the meaning of the Mass, Paul's words concerning our proclamation of the Lord's death contain much to reflect on. They open up a living of the Eucharist that is charged with great demands and expectations, which Christ's own Eucharistic example and grace, celebrated at Mass, move us to live out.

The Eucharist: Our Proclamation II

St. Paul's statement to the Christians of Corinth, "For as often as you eat this bread and drink the cup, you proclaim the Lord's death until he comes" (1 Cor 11:26), was written to a community with problems similar to our own. St. Paul touched on those difficulties as he went on to address his converts with some rather harsh words: "Now in the following instructions I do not commend you, because when you come together [at the Eucharist] it is not for the better but for the worse. For, to begin with, when you come together as a church, I hear that there are divisions among you; and to some extent I believe it.... When you come together, it is not really to eat the Lord's supper. For when the time comes to eat, each of you goes ahead with your own supper, and one goes hungry and another becomes drunk" (1 Cor 11:17, 18; 20, 21).

In those early days of the faith, Christians had a full meal when they gathered for the Eucharist. It appears that when Christians at Corinth assembled for worship they would form little cliques, taking their meals side by side. Not only were some giving scandal by overindulging, but worse still, these little groups refused to share with one another. Some who were materially well-off came with a large quantity of choice food and would not share it with others who could afford to bring only a little. St. Paul pointed out that such behavior contradicts the true meaning of the Eucharist.

He then reminded the Corinthians of the significance of the Eucharist when he asked them to remember what Jesus did at the Last Supper: how he took bread, blessed it, broke it and shared it with his disciples, saying, "This is my body that is for you. Do this in remembrance of me." By this ritual action and command Jesus invites his followers to share their lives in unconditional love after his example. Therefore, when Christians celebrate the Eucharist, in all its meaning, they are not only receiving sacramentally the grace of Jesus' saving death and presence. They are also declaring their resolve to be one with their Lord in his gift of self for the life of the world.

The Corinthians' behavior and St. Paul's response to it can move Christians of every century to ask probing questions about how they participate in their weekly Mass and live it out in everyday life. A Catholic's participation in weekly Mass is meant to result in generous self-giving and in a deep sense of unity with others. Then the celebration and living of the Eucharist will truly be "proclaiming the death of the Lord until he comes."

The Eucharist: Our Liberation I

The end of Luke's Gospel contains a marvelously rich Eucharistic text (24:13–35). It narrates how two of Jesus' disciples met their Master on the road to Emmaus, though they did not recognize him. After they had extended hospitality to him, their eyes were opened to his risen presence and his saving mission.

For the two disciples trudging along the road to Emmaus the cross was pure tragedy: "We thought Jesus' life and message was good news, but obviously they were not. We were misled. All our hopes regarding Jesus and his promise of the kingdom have come to nothing." They were walking away from Jerusalem, when they were supposed to remain there with the others. They were heading for the little village of Emmaus, and abandoning the way traced out by Jesus.

But the disciples' dejection and hopelessness were transformed, step by step, when they met a "stranger," the unrecognized Jesus. They listened to him interpret the Scripture passages referring to the Messiah, and finally invited him to spend the night with them in the inn. During their conversation with the "stranger" on the road, the disciples said they had hoped that Jesus would liberate Israel, but now those hopes had been dashed. As this narrative shows, liberation, our true freedom as God's children, is often unrecognized, even though it is a reality in our midst.

The fact of spiritual liberation, springing from God's gift of grace, and of its author, Jesus Christ, burst upon the minds of the disciples like a dawning sun when Jesus, seated at table with them, took bread, blessed it and broke it—gestures evoking the celebration of the Eucharist. In recognizing Jesus, the disciples became suddenly aware that the promise of liberation had been fulfilled for themselves and for the world.

Whenever we celebrate the Eucharist, the sacramental memorial of Jesus' dying and rising, we celebrate our spiritual freedom in God's grace. Readily do we Catholics recognize, in our "breaking of Bread," Jesus' presence and his offer of liberating grace. Perhaps we recognize Jesus less readily in the stranger whom we meet daily on the road of life—the stranger with whom Jesus has identified himself (cf. Mt 25:31–46). Yet, in recognizing Jesus in the stranger, our spiritual liberation takes root and grows into full flower.

The Eucharist: Our Liberation II

We continue our reflection on an important Eucharistic text of Luke's Gospel (24:13–35). This passage describes how two disciples, without perceiving the identity of their Master, met Jesus on the road to Emmaus and only later recognized him in the "breaking of the bread." We ask ourselves: who are the "strangers" on our road, the people we are called to see God in? God's presence in them calls forth our respect and response, but do we perhaps withhold from such persons our love, assistance and sense of justice? Are they family members or relatives we have become estranged from? Are they neighbors we turn a "cold shoulder" to because of some past misunderstanding? Are they people of other ethnic or racial groups whom we find intimidating or offensive for some reason?

These can be painful questions to ask ourselves and perhaps even more painful to answer with resolute honesty. But when we do, when we allow the grace and influence of our Eucharistic celebration to permeate our thoughts, attitudes and ideas, then we discover a wonderful sense of freedom. It opens our spiritual "eyes" to recognize the true identity of these "strangers"—their identity as sons and daughters of a heavenly Father. When we notice them, relate to them, welcome them and assist them with the mind and heart of

Christ, then we break down the walls of suspicion, mistrust and hostility. We experience a wholeness of spirit and a largeness of heart born of God's grace.

When we have thus integrated into our Christian lives the influence and effect of the Lord's sacrament, we have arrived at a celebration of the Eucharist which is truly a liberating event—an experience of our truest freedom in Christ Jesus.

The Eucharist: Our Communion

When considering the Eucharist, the word "communion" readily comes to mind with its familiar associations. However, do we reflect enough how closely communion is bound up with the Eucharist's aspects of proclamation and liberation? True spiritual liberation in the grace of Christ results in communion with God and our neighbor. Both liberation and communion are the object of Eucharistic proclamation.

The early Christian communities had a lively awareness of the Eucharist as a sacrament of communion, with its related aspects. When St. Luke described the Christian community at Jerusalem (cf. Acts 2:42–47), he portrayed these Christians as the ideal community, the one that sets the norm for all Christian communities. We are told that these Christians "devoted themselves to the apostles' teaching and fellowship, to the breaking of bread and the prayers" (Lk 2:42).

For the Jerusalem Christians their sense of oneness with Christ in the breaking of the bread, the celebration of the Eucharist, encompassed a sense of communion or fellowship with others. Their communion expressed itself in their readiness to "sell their possessions and goods and distribute the proceeds to all, as any had need" (Lk 2:45). This sense of oneness with others, with its expression of ready compassion, selflessness and charity, was so striking that it stirred many people to the depths of their being and inspired them to join the Christian community.

Further, we learn from the Acts of the Apostles and from certain of St. Paul's letters that the Christian sense of communion with others was not restricted to the local assembly. Their expressions of compassion, self-giving and charity reached beyond local and national boundaries in the form of collections taken up and distributed to poor Christian communities in distant areas of the Roman empire. These collections tell us that the early Christians recognized that the needs of others, even of those far away, called for their response. Their charity, rooted in Christ's own love, had to embrace all!

This understanding and expression of communion offers us, who often celebrate and contemplate the Eucharist, a great deal to reflect on. Perhaps it broadens our awareness of those who have a claim on our charity. Perhaps it inspires us to give generously to those frequent church collections on behalf of people in need—whether they are suffering from poverty, floods or other natural disasters. Perhaps it helps us model our love for others on the sacrificial and unitive love of the Eucharistic Christ.

May our reflections on this theme enable us to more effectively bring the grace of the Eucharist to bear upon the human thirst, often unrecognized, for God's gifts of truth, freedom and unity.

Our Unworthiness

Is it possible that in our contemporary Eucharistic thinking and practice we have lost a sense of our unworthiness before this sacrament? Certainly, it needed to be emphasized that the celebration of the Eucharist is at the vital center of our Christian life, and that the celebration ought to ordinarily include reception of the sacrament. But has this emphasis resulted, to some extent, in our taking the Eucharist for granted? Since we need it for our spiritual life, do we think it is ours by right? Has a routine of Eucharistic celebration and reception diminished our sense of attention, reverence and wonder?

The tradition of our Catholic faith is unanimous in teaching that this sacrament calls for a response of humble awe and heartfelt homage. That tradition points to individuals within salvation history who exemplified awe and homage in a memorable way. In greeting her kinswoman Mary and her yet-to-be-born Savior, Elizabeth exclaimed, "And why has this happened to me, that the mother of my Lord comes to me?" (Lk 1:43). Mary herself was troubled by the words of the angel Gabriel, because she felt unworthy of such a solemn and memorable message. The remarkable attitude of the centurion who asked Jesus to heal a household member has been immortalized, inasmuch as the Church places it before our minds every time we are offered the sacred Host: "Lord, I am not worthy to receive you, but only say the word...."

The person who approaches the Eucharistic table without recognizing his or her need for greater Christ-likeness, eats unworthily. The person who presumes that all is perfectly in order between God and neighbor and self, eats unworthily. The person who lives the Christian life minimally and thinks such living is sufficient for partaking of the Body of the Lord, eats unworthily.

When we easily and without self-examination assume that we are worthy to eat of the Eucharist, then we are in danger of succumbing to spiritual arrogance and self-sufficiency. We are in danger of closing our hearts to the grace of God, which alone can kindle our love of God and neighbor. We need to hear at every Mass the liturgy's words which remind us of our unworthiness before the Eucharistic mystery, and let these words issue from the depths of our soul: "Lord, I am not worthy to receive you, but only say the word and I shall be healed."

Our Conflicts

It is no secret that some Catholic parishes are sadly troubled by controversy, discord, resentments and ill feelings. Such a situation is truly tragic when we reflect that a Catholic parish, a community of Christians that regularly celebrates and lives from the Mass, is meant to show to the world the unity, self-giving and charity that are the grace of the Eucharist.

A parish may celebrate the Eucharist regularly and even spiritedly and yet be deaf and resistant to the claims it makes upon Christian life. The dynamism of the Eucharist is not allowed to flower in a lively, fervent charity. Selfishness, misunderstanding and conflict may take root, unpurified by the grace of the sacrament.

Christians in conflict are called to bring their problems and weaknesses to the light and influence of the Eucharist.

Because it is meant to draw all aspects of life into the mystery of Christ and the Father, this sacrament calls unceasingly for fidelity to all that Jesus wills and expects of his Church as concerns love, concord and unity.

An incomplete understanding of the Eucharist hinders us from dealing with tensions and conflicts in a truly spiritual, profound and effective way. Instead of a vision deriving from the Eucharist, we are inclined to substitute a vision based on purely human outlooks, inclinations and prejudices—on an understanding of human interaction that remains at the natural level only. Conflicts among Christians that are not brought before the sacrament of charity and unity quickly deteriorate into harsh behavior, heated exchanges, bitter judgments, stubbornness and division.

When such conflicts take root in a parish, those who strive to put the Eucharist at the center of their life and who pray often before the sacrament can be a healing and unifying influence. Their great awareness of the role of the Eucharist in Christian living and their ability to bring troubled situations to their times of prayer can help the situation. Their Eucharist-centered lives surely place them in a favored position to draw into themselves and to radiate to the community the power of the unconditional, all-embracing love that the Eucharistic Christ exemplifies and invites his followers to imitate.

Our Call to Love I

The Eucharist as the actual Body and Blood of Christ, crucified and risen for our redemption, is the absolute self-giving presence of Jesus to us. By means of this sacramental giving of himself, Jesus powerfully encourages us to respond with a gift of ourselves to him.

When this truth is deeply appreciated, our time of prayer before the Blessed Sacrament becomes a prayer to serve in love. We declare to Christ, "Lord, here I am! Receive my gift of self! Transform me! Use my life for your purposes!" Even if we fail to fathom fully its dimensions, such a prayer indicates our readiness to love with the same kind of love that he has shown us.

When our Eucharistic adoration and our sacramental Communion begin to help us take on the mind and heart of Christ, we are moved to take a new look at our relationships with all those in our daily lives, especially those who have hurt us or those whom we have hurt. This demands great sincerity, humility and honesty. But when this happens, our communion with Jesus, both sacramental and meditative, conforms our hearts to his, and strengthens us with a love that can bring forth healing and reconciliation.

If one of the effects of our Eucharistic celebration is the forgiveness of sins, it follows that our time of contemplation before the Eucharist can lead us to frequently pray: "Lord, heal us, for we have sinned against you." In that way we open ourselves to a divine healing love that dispels all hatred.

In our Eucharistic adoration we recall that the object of our praise is "the Lamb of God who takes away the sins of the world." He is our peacemaker whose universal love prevails over hatred and violence. Our prayer before the Lamb of the new pasch would be incomplete if it did not include a resolute "Lord, here I am!"—a declaration of our desire to join with the selfless charity of Christ, which animates and is at the heart of all true reconciliation and peace in our world.

Our Call to Love II

"Love one another as I have loved you" (Jn 15:12). It was not by chance that Jesus gave us that commandment during the Last Supper. For it was in the setting of that ritual meal that he instituted the Eucharist, the sacrament of his radically selfless love for the world. The Church has ever recognized that a wholehearted communion with the Eucharistic Christ at Mass necessarily entails an earnest embrace of Christ's law of love.

We cannot think that we enter into intimate communion with Christ if we do not accept the communion of charity with the needy and suffering. The needy might be the troubled family member under our roof or the terminally ill friend in a hospital, the homeless person downtown or the starving child an ocean away.

A Church that truly lives from the Eucharist knows how to express the selfless love of Christ toward all persons. The Eucharist, the sacrament of a God who loves and offers himself to draw all to him, teaches us to seek and to love our neighbor. It teaches us to transform our self-centeredness. It opens us to accept and share ourselves with the destitute and the powerless, the afflicted and the suffering. The Eucharist teaches us to embrace and heal situations of distress and pain with God's love extended through us, through our flesh and blood.

Jesus Christ, God's incarnate Love, calls us to be his presence, his voice, his hands in the midst of a society and culture tempted to ignore the needy, to satisfy selfish desires and to seek only wealth.

The Eucharistic Christ speaks powerfully of God's love for humanity—a love that we are called to enflesh in daily life. May the time that we spend in reflective prayer before the Eucharist open our minds and hearts to all that Christ wishes to teach us and accomplish in us.

Our Call to Love III

Both in our reception of the sacramental Christ at Mass and in the time we spend in reflective prayer before the Blessed Sacrament, we need to let Christ present in the Eucharist teach us! In him and through him we can overcome the lukewarmness in our relationship with God and our failures in charity toward our neighbor.

The Eucharistic Christ ever sets before us the model to follow. Our self-giving is to be nothing less than that which Jesus showed at the Last Supper, when he bent down to wash the feet of his disciples, when he broke bread in an act of total self-giving for the salvation of all. In living out this example of selfless love, we build up the Church, the body of Christ. We fulfill our vocation of being a living temple of praise of God, and we become a center of light, hope and service to others.

When we weave into our lives regular times of prayer before the Eucharist, we have privileged occasions to contemplate lovingly and to learn from him who is both our traveling companion and our food for the difficult journey.

These times of prayer also offer us precious moments for fervent petition. We can ask Christ to illuminate his Church with his powerful light and grace, to help it reject the lure of materialism, and to defeat the selfishness that threatens it, the injustices that upset it, the divisions that menace it.

In every aspect of his Eucharistic self-giving to us,

Christ wants us to live from the inexhaustible love of his heart. May we adore God with ardent affection, and serve others with an ever attentive and active charity.

Celebrating a Fruitful Eucharist

The New Testament's earliest written account of the institution of the Eucharist appears in chapter 11 of First Corinthians. Yet, in the midst of this splendid testimony, we hear Paul reproach the Corinthians for failing to comprehend the real significance of what they celebrated. In failing in charity and moderation at their fraternal supper, during which the Eucharist was celebrated, this community of Christians confused their human purposes with the divine. As a consequence, they became divided, weakened and in danger of dying. "For all who eat and drink without discerning the body, eat and drink judgment against themselves" (1 Cor 11:29).

St. Paul had good reason to reprove them, for he saw clearly enough that the Eucharist, and everything that concerns this sacrament, cannot be used for selfish interests. It calls for an undivided heart and a gift of self, because its objective is to form the one body of Christ, who is ever the undivided one as human history unfolds in time and moves to its end.

What does all this mean for us as we go about our daily lives and as we regularly celebrate the Eucharist? Does it not mean that we would often deserve St. Paul's rebuke: "In this matter I do not commend you" (1 Cor 11:22)? Doesn't truth compel us to admit that our participation in the Eucharist is too often routine, listless and unfruitful, because our spiritual dispositions are wanting? We may approach the Lord's Supper lacking the serious intent to measure our lives against Christ's word and example. We may celebrate the Eucharist to do something expected of us, something religiously satisfying, and not to let Christ challenge us by the total gift he makes of himself and by all he exemplifies in the Eucharist. In embracing this challenge we will truly share the fruitfulness of this sacrament.

The one who redeemed the world by giving over his will totally to the Father, putting himself completely at his disposal, asks that in every celebration of Mass and in our hours of prayer before the Eucharist we renounce the selfishness within us so as to become true children of God and loving brothers and sisters, in Christ, to all people.

Model of Our Mission

If Catholic evangelization is to be effective, we need to continually contemplate the charity of Christ present in the Eucharist. The Church discovers there the true character of its charity—a charity that constantly goes beyond community limits to extend itself to all people, whom Christ loves and whom he wishes to draw into his love for the Father.

Such charity calls for a Christian community that is not self-centered in regard to its projects, institutions or needs. Its center of life and mission is always to be the Eucharistic Christ. In drawing from the power of this sacrament, the Church can comprehend clearly its mission toward each person and situation that needs to be reached and transformed by the good news of Christ.

The Eucharist is the paradigm, the model before which

the Church kneels in contemplation, and against which the Church assesses its life and activity. This is needed if the Church is to fulfill both its missionary vocation and its call to witness before the world a life that is truly drawn into Christ's love for the Father, a life that is thereby brought to true human fulfillment.

We members of the Church are to understand that the needs of our brethren are not the ultimate criterion of mission. That criterion is our sharing of the love of Christ and of his love of the Father. This love impels us to search out and seek to meet urgent human needs. This love enables us to uncover the true depths and dimensions of human needs, revealing what is simply inadequate and superficial about various proposed solutions.

Christ's paschal love, the love he displayed for the Father and for the world in his act of redemption, is set continually before the Church for its contemplation and emulation. This love alone can keep our missionary vision in true focus and regenerate our energies to faithfully proclaim Christ's good news.

Heart of Evangelization I

Despite our strong emphasis on the sacramental Body of Christ in our liturgical and devotional life, perhaps we Catholics think that the core of evangelization is inspired preaching of the Gospel or effective sharing of the Scriptures. But the true life-giving, animating center of Catholic evangelization is the Eucharist.

This is self-evident when we recall that Catholic evangelization is directed to inviting people to the full experience of Jesus Christ as he is proclaimed, celebrated and given in the liturgy of the Eucharist and especially in Holy Communion. When Jesus feeds us with his Body in the Eucharist, his Holy Spirit continues forming us into his body, the Church. The Church in turn continues gathering the harvest of the human family into the banquet of God's kingdom.

To speak of the Eucharist is to speak of Jesus Christ—the one who is from the Father and ever lives for the Father in the Holy Spirit—in a way that includes the world which the Father has chosen to create in, with and through him. Through the Incarnation, Jesus Christ entered all aspects of worldly reality—its joys, its sufferings, its burden of sin (without sinning himself)—for the purpose of gathering creation into the relationship of love he has with the Father and the Holy Spirit.

Jesus comes forth from the Father to gather up and free humanity in order that it may participate in his eternal love. Through Baptism and the Eucharist, Christians receive the reality of Jesus Christ, and are thereby inserted into his self-emptying love—a love that ever extends itself to all, pours itself out for the sake of all.

Christians have a mission to extend the reality of Christ into the world, and thereby to contribute to the world's sanctification. In carrying out their mission, they transmit to the world around them the love of Christ which they have received and which continually vivifies them through the liturgy and sacraments of the Church, in an altogether preeminent way through the Eucharist.

Heart of Evangelization II

Evangelization is an integral aspect of Pope John Paul II's repeated call to Christians to bring about a "civilization of love." In his encyclical *Mission of the Redeemer,* he says that "'works of charity' reveal the soul of all missionary activity; love, which has been and remains the driving force of mission, is the principle which must direct every action and the end to which that action must be directed" (n. 60). The dynamic, the "soul" that animates evangelization, is love, a love that is modeled on and nurtured by Jesus' utterly selfless, sacrificial love. In the celebration of Mass and in Eucharist-related times of prayer, we constantly grow in communion with this love.

If love inspired and nurtured by the Eucharist is the "soul" of evangelization, the Christian's witness to others cannot be a hard-sell proselytizing, but one marked by true discretion and prudence. However, these virtues have nothing to do with a soulless, indifferent "niceness," but are to embody a life of witness that springs from the grace of Christ. It means allowing a true Christ-like love to take hold of and guide our dealings with the many people we meet in daily life.

Finally, it's good to realize that we cannot measure our evangelizing efforts against this world's standards of success. Our model here, as always, is Jesus Christ, who entered and transformed our world by way of the cross. As co-workers with Christ through Baptism and the Eucharist, our way is also that of the cross. The cross, however, contains the seed of resurrection, as the Eucharist ever proclaims to us and implants within us.

Eucharistic Presence I

Down through the centuries the Catholic Church has lived by the conviction that it correctly interprets the intention of Jesus when it worships him in his Eucharistic presence. Besides the judgment of the Church's leadership in this matter, the massive devotional response of the faithful is a decisive criterion for concluding that the Church acts under the guidance of the Holy Spirit.

From the testimony of Scripture, we see how Jesus gave the altogether new reality of the Eucharist to his disciples in the simplest of statements. Down through the centuries, the Church contemplates this reality and draws from it an ever greater understanding and devotional response. This is true for the sacrificial aspect of the Eucharist as well as for the aspect of Christ's presence.

Beginning in the Middle Ages the Church, especially in the West, discerned in the intention of Christ a sure, though implicit, foundation for worship of the Eucharist beyond the liturgy of the Mass. Since the Eucharistic presence of Christ continues after the offering and the act of Communion, its permanence prolongs the effect of the sacrifice and Holy Communion.

When we desire to join ourselves more intensely with the offering of the Mass and to renew our personal contact with Christ enjoyed at the time of Communion, we instinctively turn toward that enduring presence of Christ reserved in our churches and chapels. This will rekindle our charity at the source of the Church's unity. By calling forth our loving presence in response, the Eucharistic presence of Christ tends to become the center of our individual lives as it is the center of the Church's life.

When we kneel before the Eucharist, the Lord helps us understand the full meaning of this sacrament: it unites our personal offering to that of Christ; it transforms our lives through Communion with the Bread of Life; it calls us to give our love, in adoring contemplation, in response to the love that Jesus' Eucharistic presence embodies and reveals.

Eucharistic Presence II

Christ prolongs his sacramental presence beyond the Eucharistic celebration to bring about a deeper spiritual communion with the individual Christian. But this truth also has a wider dimension, namely, that Christ wishes to strengthen spiritual communion with the entire Church. His abiding sacramental presence nourishes the life of the whole Mystical Body.

The early Christians often lovingly dwelt on the truth that the Church is founded on the Eucharistic presence of Christ. The members of the Church are truly united by this sacramental bond that joins them to the Savior. This truth is simply yet splendidly expressed in the image of the vine and the branches (cf. Jn 15:1–5). It is surely correct to assume that when Jesus used this striking image, he was thinking of the Eucharist. The image of the vine and the branches helps us understand the hidden yet powerful effect on those who drink the consecrated Wine, the Blood of the new covenant.

However, the influence that the Eucharistic Christ has on the Mystical Body does not stop at the moment of Communion. The Eucharist is an abiding presence in the Church that constantly influences the hearts of its members and communicates to them the power of charity.

This sacramental reality contains Christ's presence within the Mystical Body. In the reserved sacrament, he remains as the source of love for the community he founded. The abiding Eucharistic presence vividly shows how Christ resides at the center of a particular community of Christians. This manner of presence allows a wondrous multiplication of Christ's presence in many places, making that presence more concrete and more accessible. It shows that his love wishes to extend itself into every Christian community to forge and strengthen the bonds of charity.

As we pray before the Eucharist and allow the truth of all this to come to mind, it will stir within us fervent praise and thanksgiving. This abiding Eucharistic presence, always vivifying the life of the Mystical Body, gives a full sense to those consoling words of Jesus: "Remember, I am with you always, to the end of the age" (Mt 28:20).

Eucharistic Presence III

"Nor is the [Eucharistic] sacrament to be less the object of adoration because it was instituted by Christ the Lord to be received as food." These words from the *Instruction on the Worship of the Eucharistic Mystery* (no. 3), issued shortly after Vatican II, reveal the Church's concern that the abiding Eucharistic presence, the worship it invites, and Eucharistic Communion be seen as truly complementary aspects of the sacrament. When Christ gives himself under the appearances of bread and wine, he evidently intends that it should lead to Communion. However, this does not mean that the abiding Eucharistic presence has no further function or significance within the Christian's spiritual life.

In giving himself to us as food, Christ gives his life to us in such a way that, ideally, helps us to live the divine life ever more intently. Eucharistic Communion is aimed at completely uniting us to Christ in faith and love. This is certainly achieved in a frequent and fervent reception of the Lord's Body. But the union of spirit and the intimate dialogue of love that take place in the act of Communion are meant to be prolonged beyond the celebration of Mass. The abiding Eucharistic presence and the periodic focusing of our prayer and attention upon it can serve to extend throughout the day the loving exchange that unfolds at Communion.

When we come before Christ's sacramental presence, we can renew our union with him through acts of love, faith and hope—just as we did at the time of Communion. We can continue, in a more prolonged and contemplative fashion, the spiritual communing with Christ that followed reception of the Eucharist.

Through his abiding Eucharistic presence, Christ continues to nourish us spiritually even after the brief moments of actual sacramental Communion. He asks for our adoration and love, and invites us to ongoing spiritual communion. The abiding Eucharistic presence of Christ allows our Communion with him at Mass to completely encompass and fill our Christian existence.

Exploring the Riches of the Eucharist I

The mystery of the Eucharist, approached in a spirit of contemplation and adoration, invites us to explore the great variety and wonder of its riches. These riches are discovered in Jesus' intention in instituting the Eucharist, as well as in the Church's ongoing understanding and experience of the Eucharist.

What was Jesus' intention in instituting the sacrament of his Body and Blood? Jesus' words, by which he gave himself to his disciples and to his Church under the signs of bread and wine, certainly speak of eating and drinking, and, on a deeper level, of personal communion. Yet, we must say that Communion does not exhaust the significance of Christ's presence.

The words by which Jesus gave his sacred Body and Blood reveal that he placed these realities in relation to his sacrifice on Calvary. He said, "This is my body, which is given for you. Do this in remembrance of me" (Lk 22:19), and again, "This is my blood of the covenant, which is poured out for many" (Mk 14:24). These words of Jesus put his Body and Blood in relation to a sacrifice before they are given in a meal. In a manner completely beyond human comprehension, Jesus anticipated his self-offering on Calvary, making present his Body and Blood in their sacrificial condition.

The Body and Blood of Christ must first embody his saving sacrifice, must first contain his redemptive presence, before they can be nourishment "for many," "for the life of the world" (Jn 6:51). The presence of Jesus, in his self-offering sacramentally given, gives meaning to the food and drink that Jesus gives us.

Our prayer before the Eucharist, and more importantly our reception of the Eucharist, is ever an occasion to lovingly recognize the body of the Lord (cf. 1 Cor 11:29). This real presence gives value to our "sacrifice of praise" and ensures the Church's unity, charity and sanctification—the effects of Eucharistic Communion. "Hidden God, devoutly I adore you, truly present underneath these veils. All my heart subdues itself before you, since to fathom you it faints and fails" (*Adoro Te Devote,* St. Thomas Aquinas).

Exploring the Riches of the Eucharist II

The Catholic Church always reminds us that when we pray before the Eucharistic sacrament, we encounter the very person of Christ. At the Last Supper Jesus gave his disciples bread and declared it to be his body. It is likely that the Aramaic word he used to express this meant "flesh," meaning the entirety of his self, his whole person. Thus, what Jesus gives to his disciples and to us in the Eucharist is the gift of his entire personal being.

Reflection on this tremendous mystery moves us to respond to Christ's Eucharistic gift of self with the reciprocal gift of our whole person. In other words, when we come to Mass and to pray before the Blessed Sacrament, we bring not only our physical presence, posture and voice, but also our attention, thought, reflection and affection.

The very personal aspect of Jesus' Eucharistic presence is not simply of secondary importance, but was central to Jesus' intention as he instituted the Eucharist. As he prepared to leave his little band of disciples and to embrace his redemptive sacrifice, he instituted a sacrament that grants them access, not only to the grace of that sacrifice, but also to himself, the victim of the sacrifice. Jesus gave to his disciples, and through them to his Church, a new presence that would prolong for all time the intimacy he wishes to have with his own. Jesus' Eucharistic presence, corporal and personal, truly perpetuates the presence of his Incarnation.

Recalling in this light the words of his Last Supper discourse, we can appreciate the full extent of Jesus' promise to remain with his faithful ones (cf. Jn 15:4–10). When he spoke of "remaining," Jesus seemed to be pointing to the Eucharist's effects of grace. The ritual act of departure inaugurates a new personal presence of Christ for all ages to come.

How are we to respond to this personal presence of Christ sacramentally given? How can we "remain" in this gift of his love? As the Church encourages us, it is by praying before the Eucharistic Christ, and it is also by finding and serving Christ in the great variety of people who daily come into our lives. Jesus assures us that when we give to another human being the gift of ourselves with a charity nourished on the Eucharist, we truly remain in him. "This is my commandment, that you love one another as I have loved you. If you keep my commandments, you will abide in my love" (Jn 15:12, 10).

Exploring the Riches of the Eucharist III

The sacrament of the Eucharist, which often touches our lives in public worship, Communion and private prayer, wondrously attests to the divine power residing in the humanity of Jesus Christ. As Son of God, Jesus exercises this power when he gives his Body to be eaten and his Blood to be drunk. He can actualize the consecration of the bread and the wine because of the power that he holds over created being. He holds this power because he is, himself, absolute being—one with God, with the Father and the Holy Spirit.

Through the Incarnation and the Eucharist, Jesus Christ establishes his active and faithful presence in the midst of humanity. His absolute presence will never fail the humanity he has redeemed and the Church he has brought into being. His Eucharistic presence fulfills in the most astonishing manner possible his promise to his disciples: "I am with you always, to the end of the age" (Mt 28:20).

The divine presence and power, abiding always in Jesus Christ and extended into time and space through the Eucharist, permits Jesus to be "spirit and life" for his disciples. But the divine riches of the Eucharist are accessible only through an absolute faith—a fact that Jesus underscored (cf. Jn 6:61–68). One cannot be nourished by the "bread come down from heaven" without faith in the divine presence and power it contains.

But what is required of us once we fully acknowledge by faith the divine presence of Jesus in the Eucharist? The answer is adoration. Christ asks us to join ourselves to him in his Eucharistic offering and to receive him lovingly in sacramental Communion. In giving us his altogether unique presence in the Eucharist, he also invites us to adore him. Without this adoration, the Eucharistic offering could not be recognized in all its sublimity, and the banquet of Communion could not have its full value. According to the famous statement of St. Augustine: "No one eats this flesh if he has not first adored it."

The adoration that we bring to the Eucharistic presence is not directed to a thing but to a Person. It is love discerning and embracing Jesus who is Lord and God.

Resurrection I

Our celebration of the Eucharist is central to our celebration of Easter, for the Eucharist captures and extends to us sacramentally the full redemptive sweep of Jesus' dying and rising. Not only our Easter Eucharist, but also every celebration of Mass puts us in touch with the saving Christ and enables us to join him in bringing the world to its God-intended wholeness.

Because the Eucharist contains the actual presence of the risen Christ, it points toward the fulfillment of God's kingdom. The risen Christ prefigures a renewed creation. Therefore, the Eucharist not only looks to what Christ did in the past for our world but also to what he will do, and is even now doing, for the world.

The sacramental Christ does indeed speak to us of a transfigured creation, a world made to share in his resurrection. But even more, he involves us in the process of that transfiguration by giving us his very self to eat and calling us to daily live his example of selfless love. Each day, in our personal relationship to God and our dealings with others, there are "dyings" to be offered, obstacles to be cleared, battles to be won, new structures to be built. However, rooted in Christ's grace and nourished with his Body, we struggle and work and live with the life of the resurrection already pulsating in our being. For all their brushes with occasional darkness and failure, our Christian lives carry within them something of the paschal victory that the Eucharist announces and nurtures.

Resurrection II

The Church's celebration of Easter draws our attention not only to Christ's resurrection, but also to our resurrection, which is rooted in his. Our reflections on the Easter mystery center not only on Christ's promise of our resurrection (cf. Jn 11:25), but also on the gift of his Eucharistic self as the dynamic principle of resurrected life: "Those who eat my flesh and drink my blood have eternal life, and I will raise them up on the last day" (Jn 6:54).

The Eucharist, which communicates to us here and now Jesus' own life, also guarantees the fullness of divine life to be bestowed after death. The risen body of Jesus, given to us in the Eucharist, empowers our whole being, body and soul, and prepares us to share in the fullness of life that is resurrection.

Perhaps we need to appreciate more deeply the depth of the risen Lord's Eucharistic gift of self. It communicates to us not only the life of Christ, but also, and necessarily, that of the Trinity. In the Eucharist the glorified Christ ever receives life from the Father, in the unity of the Holy Spirit, before communicating that same life to us: "Just as the living Father sent me, and I live because of the Father, so whoever eats me will live because of me" (Jn 6:57).

What a wondrous mystery to savor and welcome as we eat of the Eucharist and pray in its presence! Divine life issues ceaselessly from the Father, infuses the risen Son and flows out upon his Church, communicated through his Eucharistic gift of self. This divine life, trinitarian and Eucharistic, will eventually bring about the miracle of our resurrection in Christ.

When we grasp this truth, we can more deeply appreciate the Eucharist as that vital factor in a process that begins within our present Christian life and will culminate after our death. The Eucharist, the sacramental Body of the risen Lord and the "food of wayfarers," sublimely heralds our resurrection because Christ, who is ever faithful to his promises, has pledged that those who eat his flesh will not perish but will be raised up and live forever.

Christ the Lord I

Although the Son of God was ever one with the Father and the Holy Spirit in sovereignty over creation, in his human nature he chose to "acquire" the title of Lord and King. The Lordship of Jesus is far removed from earthly concepts of royalty, power and dominion. His reign is founded on and is exercised in love alone. Jesus lived his entire life in loving service of others—a service that culminated when he poured out his life on Calvary. In Jesus' resurrection and glorification, the Father crowned this service of love with the honor of lordship (cf. Phil 2:8–11).

Jesus rendered this service of love to the world in the midst of struggle. In his teaching, comforting and healing ministry Jesus took on the forces of evil—the darkness, blindness and ignorance that grip the lives of men and women. Jesus engaged the malign influences that ravage the Godlike image which persons are meant to reflect in their being.

The culminating act of love and self-giving which Jesus made on Calvary is captured in the Eucharist, the sacrament of Calvary's love made present and accessible to us here and now. When Jesus celebrated the first Eucharist, he proclaimed his commandment of love, the fundamental, all-embracing law of his kingdom, and exemplified it in all clarity and greatness. He decreed, "I give you a new commandment, that you love one another. Just as I have loved you, you also should love one another" (Jn 13:34). He proceeded to give his chosen disciples, and to all humanity, his whole self, Body and Blood, in this sacrament. He then directed his disciples, "Do this in remembrance of me" (Lk 22:19).

Our Eucharistic prayer can lead us to make a sincere gift of self in love after the example of Jesus. Christian love could not exist in all its authenticity and vibrancy without the Eucharist. The Eucharist inspires and nourishes the love by which Christians become true citizens of Christ's kingdom, and by means of love they effectively announce and extend the reign of Jesus in the world.

Christ the Lord II

In the Gospels, especially in John, the kingship of Jesus comes to light even in his passion and crucifixion. The soldiers mockingly clothed Jesus with a purple mantle and a crown of thorns, and greeted him with the title "King of the Jews." The religious authorities, unexpectedly recognizing the hated Roman emperor, accused Jesus of rival claims to kingship. An inscription nailed to the cross announced scornfully, "Jesus of Nazareth, King of the Jews." In Jesus' utter abasement, his majesty was revealed.

The wooden cross, the crown of thorns, the iron nails have long ceased to play their awful role, but the self-offering of Jesus endures sacramentally, and pleads to the Father on behalf of a graceless, resisting, scoffing world. Upon the altar of sacrifice this Savior-King comes to his people to communicate to them, through all ages, the effective grace of his sacrifice, and to implant in them the spirit of his kingdom.

Through the bountiful grace of the Eucharist Jesus wishes to be enthroned as king within our heart, as Lord over our life. May the many thoughts, words and actions that fill each day proclaim the sovereignty of Jesus over our whole life. Every time we open our mind, heart and soul to the Eucharist's healing, saving and transforming effect, we further the reign of Christ in the world. But the kingdom of Christ is, in a sense, incomplete as long as there are minds that reject his word, hearts that refuse his rule, persons who resist his grace.

May we daily open wide our hearts and lives to Jesus, Redeemer and King. May we so fervently celebrate the Eucharist and adore the Savior we receive that our lives may always more powerfully witness to his kingdom and extend his reign in our troubled world.

Christ the Lord III

The "apostle of the Eucharist," St. Peter Julian Eymard, never tired of repeating—and correctly so—that the kingship of Christ is founded and exercised wholly on love. The reign of even the most devoted and beneficent sovereign cannot compare to Christ's, for Jesus alone can know personally every one of his disciples. Jesus alone can know and satisfy the most intimate needs of his people.

The laws of Christ's kingdom have their origin and

revelation from love alone. Far from being arbitrary and restrictive rules of conduct, the laws of Christ manifest God's eternal will and love—a will and love directed entirely to the human person's fulfillment in grace. As founder and Lord of this new reign of grace, Jesus accomplishes what the prophet Jeremiah predicted: that in the New Covenant the laws of God would be planted deep within the human person and written on the heart. "But this is the covenant that I will make with the house of Israel after those days, says the Lord: I will put my law within them, and I will write it on their hearts; and I will be their God, and they shall be my people" (Jer 31:33).

This implanting and inscribing of the laws of the New Covenant is formed in Jesus' sacrificial body and blood. For St. Peter Julian, this implanting takes place most effectively when, with a ready and generous love, we receive the Lord's sacramental Body and Blood: "Here, by means of the sacrament, he himself comes to write his law in our hearts. Within the heart of the communicant he inscribes the law of holiness and truth. He inscribes, not with his hands but with his heart, giving proof of his love for us in order to communicate to us his ways, his divine life, that we might live of the very life of God himself."

Through the Eucharist may we always place ourselves freely and lovingly under Christ's reign of grace. By drawing from his Eucharistic gift of self, may we, submitting our minds and hearts to his loving will, persevere in his kingdom and finally attain that blessedness in which we shall abide with him, the Father and the Holy Spirit forever.

Mary: A Presence Ever Near

"All these were constantly devoting themselves to prayer, together with certain women, including Mary the mother of Jesus, as well as his brothers.... They devoted themselves to the apostles' teaching and fellowship, to the breaking of bread and the prayers" (Acts 1:14; 2:42). With these few phrases, Luke, the author of the Acts of the Apostles, gave us a concise and wonderful glimpse into the life of the early Christian Church. He purposely stated that Mary, the Mother of Jesus, was present and active in the life of the Church.

Gathered with Mary, those first Christians lived in eager attentiveness to the teachings of the apostles, in fervent prayer and worship, in profound joy and peace, and in active charity toward all. They sought to bring about in their lives all that the "breaking of Bread," the celebration of the Eucharist, the sacrament of unity and charity, was meant to achieve.

In the midst of these first Christians, Mary surely exercised an important influence both by her prayers and example, which helped the community become everything that her Son expected it to be.

Down through the centuries, the Church has continually looked to Mary as a model for our Christian lives, who shows us how to live as disciples. We see her close association with her Son's apostles and her receptiveness to their teaching, and we learn how to be open to our Church's leaders and teachers. We see her fervent reverence and worship, and we learn how to adore. We see her profound joy and peace in the Lord, and we learn how to acquire these fruits of the Spirit. We see her participate in the lively charity of the early Christians, and we learn how to share of ourselves and our goods with all people.

Our Catholic Church lives with the abiding conviction that Mary is still in our midst, still present with us as we "break the Bread," as we celebrate the Eucharist. (Every Eucharistic Prayer commemorates the Virgin Mother of God.) Mary continues to show us how to nourish in ourselves all that the Eucharist is meant to bring about. By her example and never ceasing prayers, Mary continues to assist us in becoming more authentically the Eucharistic Church of her Son.

Appendix

These Scriptural passages can be used
for prayerful reflection before the Blessed Sacrament.

The Bread of Life Discourse
John 6:22–59

> The next day the crowd that had stayed on the other side of the sea saw that there had been only one boat there. They also saw that Jesus had not got into the boat with his disciples, but that his disciples had gone away alone. Then some boats from Tiberias came near the place where they had eaten the bread after the Lord had given thanks. So when the crowd saw that neither Jesus nor his disciples were there, they themselves got into the boats and went to Capernaum looking for Jesus.
>
> When they found him on the other side of the sea, they said to him, "Rabbi, when did you come here?" Jesus answered them, "Very truly, I tell you, you are looking for me, not because you saw signs, but because you ate your fill of the loaves. Do not work for the food that perishes, but for the food that endures for eternal life, which the Son of Man will give you. For it is on him that God the Father has set his seal." Then they said to him, "What must we do to perform the works of God?" Jesus answered them,

"This is the work of God, that you believe in him whom he has sent." So they said to him, "What sign are you going to give us then, so that we may see it and believe you? What work are you performing? Our ancestors ate the manna in the wilderness; as it is written, 'He gave them bread from heaven to eat.'" Then Jesus said to them, "Very truly, I tell you, it was not Moses who gave you the bread from heaven, but it is my Father who gives you the true bread from heaven. For the bread of God is that which comes down from heaven and gives life to the world." They said to him, "Sir, give us this bread always."

Jesus said to them, "I am the bread of life. Whoever comes to me will never be hungry, and whoever believes in me will never be thirsty. But I said to you that you have seen me and yet do not believe. Everything that the Father gives me will come to me, and anyone who comes to me I will never drive away; for I have come down from heaven, not to do my own will, but the will of him who sent me. And this is the will of him who sent me, that I should lose nothing of all that he has given me, but raise it up on the last day. This is indeed the will of my Father, that all who see the Son and believe in him may have eternal life; and I will raise them up on the last day."

Then the Jews began to complain about him because he said, "I am the bread that came down from heaven." They were saying, "Is not this Jesus, the son of Joseph, whose father and mother we know? How can he now say, 'I have come down from heaven'?" Jesus answered them, "Do not complain among yourselves. No one can come to me unless drawn by the Father who sent me; and I will raise that person up on the last day. It is written in the prophets, 'And they shall all be taught by God.' Everyone who has heard and learned from the Father comes to me. Not that anyone has seen the Father except the one who is from God; he has seen the Father. Very truly, I tell you, whoever believes has eternal life. I am the bread of life. Your ancestors ate the manna in the wilderness, and they died. This is the bread that comes down from heaven, so that one may eat of it and not die. I am the living bread that came down from heaven. Whoever eats of this bread will live forever; and the bread that I will give for the life of the world is my flesh."

The Jews then disputed among themselves, saying, "How can this man give us his flesh to eat?" So Jesus said to them, "Very truly, I tell you, unless you eat the flesh of the Son of Man and drink his blood, you have no life in you. Those who eat my flesh and drink my blood have eternal life, and I will raise them up on the last day; for my flesh is true food and my blood is true drink. Those who eat my flesh and drink my blood abide in me, and I in them. Just as the living Father sent me, and I live because of the Father, so whoever eats me will live because of me. This is the bread that came down from heaven, not like that which your ancestors ate, and they died. But the one who eats this bread will live forever." He said these things while he was teaching in the synagogue at Capernaum.

Words of Institution of the Eucharist
Matthew 26:26–29

> While they were eating, Jesus took a loaf of bread, and after blessing it he broke it, gave it to the disciples, and said, "Take, eat; this is my body." Then he took a cup, and after giving thanks he gave it to them, saying, "Drink from it, all of you; for this is my blood of the covenant, which is poured out for many for the forgiveness of sins. I tell you, I will never again drink of this fruit of the vine until that day when I drink it new with you in my Father's kingdom."

Luke 22:19–20

> Then he took a loaf of bread, and when he had given thanks, he broke it and gave it to them, saying, "This is my body, which is given for you. Do this in remembrance of me." And he did the same with the cup after supper, saying, "This cup that is poured out for you is the new covenant in my blood."

The Grain of Wheat
John 12:20–36

> Now among those who went up to worship at the festival were some Greeks. They came to Philip, who was from Bethsaida in Galilee, and said to him, "Sir, we wish to see Jesus." Philip went and told Andrew; then Andrew and Philip went and told Jesus. Jesus answered them, "The hour has come for the Son of Man to be glorified. Very truly, I tell you, unless a grain of wheat falls into the earth and dies, it

remains just a single grain; but if it dies, it bears much fruit. Those who love their life lose it, and those who hate their life in this world will keep it for eternal life. Whoever serves me must follow me, and where I am, there will my servant be also. Whoever serves me, the Father will honor.

"Now my soul is troubled. And what should I say—'Father, save me from this hour'? No, it is for this reason that I have come to this hour. Father, glorify your name." Then a voice came from heaven, "I have glorified it, and I will glorify it again." The crowd standing there heard it and said that it was thunder. Others said, "An angel has spoken to him." Jesus answered, "This voice has come for your sake, not for mine. Now is the judgment of this world; now the ruler of this world will be driven out. And I, when I am lifted up from the earth, will draw all people to myself." He said this to indicate the kind of death he was to die. The crowd answered him, "We have heard from the law that the Messiah remains forever. How can you say that the Son of Man must be lifted up? Who is this Son of Man?" Jesus said to them, "The light is with you for a little longer. Walk while you have the light, so that the darkness may not overtake you. If you walk in the darkness, you do not know where you are going. While you have the light, believe in the light, so that you may become children of light."

The Road to Emmaus
Luke 24:13–35

> Now on that same day two of them were going to a village called Emmaus, about seven miles from Jerusalem, and talking with each other about all these things that had happened. While they were talking and discussing, Jesus himself came near and went with them, but their eyes were kept from recognizing him. And he said to them, "What are you discussing with each other while you walk along?" They stood still, looking sad. Then one of them, whose name was Cleopas, answered him, "Are you the only stranger in Jerusalem who does not know the things that have taken place there in these days?" He asked them, "What things?" They replied, "The things about Jesus of Nazareth, who was a prophet mighty in deed and word before God and all the people, and how our chief priests and leaders handed him over to be condemned to death and crucified him. But we had hoped that he was the one to redeem Israel. Yes, and besides all this, it is now the third day since these things took place. Moreover, some women of our group astounded us. They were at the tomb early this morning, and when they did not find his body there, they came back and told us that they had indeed seen a vision of angels who said that he was alive. Some of those who were with us went to the tomb and found it just as the women had said; but they did not see him." Then he said to them, "Oh, how foolish you are, and how slow of heart to believe all that the prophets have declared! Was it not necessary that the Messiah should suffer these things

and then enter into his glory?" Then beginning with Moses and all the prophets, he interpreted to them the things about himself in all the scriptures.

As they came near the village to which they were going, he walked ahead as if he were going on. But they urged him strongly, saying, "Stay with us, because it is almost evening and the day is now nearly over." So he went in to stay with them. When he was at the table with them, he took bread, blessed and broke it, and gave it to them. Then their eyes were opened, and they recognized him; and he vanished from their sight. They said to each other, "Were not our hearts burning within us while he was talking to us on the road, while he was opening the scriptures to us?" That same hour they got up and returned to Jerusalem; and they found the eleven and their companions gathered together. They were saying, "The Lord has risen indeed, and he has appeared to Simon!" Then they told what had happened on the road, and how he had been made known to them in the breaking of the bread.

Life of the Early Disciples

Acts 2:42–47

They devoted themselves to the apostles' teaching and fellowship, to the breaking of bread and the prayers. Awe came upon everyone, because many wonders and signs were being done by the apostles. All who believed were together and had all things in common; they would sell their possessions and goods and distribute the proceeds to all, as any had need. Day by day, as they spent much time together in the temple, they broke bread at home and ate their food with glad and generous hearts, praising God and having the goodwill of all the people. And day by day the Lord added to their number those who were being saved.

Jesus the True Vine
John 15:1–11

"I am the true vine, and my Father is the vinegrower. He removes every branch in me that bears no fruit. Every branch that bears fruit he prunes to make it bear more fruit. You have already been cleansed by the word that I have spoken to you. Abide in me as I abide in you. Just as the branch cannot bear fruit by itself unless it abides in the vine, neither can you unless you abide in me. I am the vine, you are the branches. Those who abide in me and I in them bear much fruit, because apart from me you can do nothing. Whoever does not abide in me is thrown away like a branch and withers; such branches are gathered, thrown into the fire, and burned. If you abide in me, and my words abide in you, ask for whatever you wish, and it will be done for you. My Father is glorified by this, that you bear much fruit and become my disciples. As the Father has loved me, so I have loved you; abide in my love. If you keep my commandments, you will abide in my love, just as I have kept my Father's commandments and abide in his love. I have said these things to you so that my joy may be in you, and that your joy may be complete.

Jesus Is the Resurrection and the Life
John 11:25–26

> Jesus said to her, "I am the resurrection and the life. Those who believe in me, even though they die, will live, and everyone who lives and believes in me will never die."

The Lordship of Jesus
Phil 2:5–11

> Let the same mind be in you that was in Christ Jesus, who, though he was in the form of God, did not regard equality with God as something to be exploited, but emptied himself, taking the form of a slave, being born in human likeness. And being found in human form, he humbled himself and became obedient to the point of death—even death on a cross. Therefore God also highly exalted him and gave him the name that is above every name, so that at the name of Jesus every knee should bend, in heaven and on earth and under the earth, and every tongue should confess that Jesus Christ is Lord, to the glory of God the Father.

BOOKS & MEDIA

The Daughters of St. Paul operate book and media centers at the following addresses. Visit, call or write the one nearest you today, or find us on the World Wide Web, www.pauline.org

California
3908 Sepulveda Blvd., Culver City, CA 90230; 310-397-8676
5945 Balboa Ave., San Diego, CA 92111; 619-565-9181
46 Geary Street, San Francisco, CA 94108; 415-781-5180

Florida
145 S.W. 107th Ave., Miami, FL 33174; 305-559-6715

Hawaii
1143 Bishop Street, Honolulu, HI 96813; 808-521-2731

Illinois
172 North Michigan Ave., Chicago, IL 60601; 312-346-4228

Louisiana
4403 Veterans Memorial Blvd., Metairie, LA 70006; 504-887-7631

Massachusetts
Rte. 1, 885 Providence Hwy., Dedham, MA 02026; 781-326-5385

Missouri
9804 Watson Rd., St. Louis, MO 63126; 314-965-3512

New Jersey
561 U.S. Route 1, Wick Plaza, Edison, NJ 08817; 732-572-1200

New York
150 East 52nd Street, New York, NY 10022; 212-754-1110
78 Fort Place, Staten Island, NY 10301; 718-447-5071

Ohio
2105 Ontario Street, Cleveland, OH 44115; 216-621-9427

Pennsylvania
9171-A Roosevelt Blvd., Philadelphia, PA 19114; 215-676-9494

South Carolina
243 King Street, Charleston, SC 29401; 843-577-0175

Tennessee
4811 Poplar Ave., Memphis, TN 38117; 901-761-2987

Texas
114 Main Plaza, San Antonio, TX 78205; 210-224-8101

Virginia
1025 King Street, Alexandria, VA 22314; 703-549-3806

Canada
3022 Dufferin Street, Toronto, Ontario, Canada M6B 3T5; 416-781-9131
1155 Yonge Street, Toronto, Ontario, Canada M4T 1W2; 416-934-3440

¡Libros en español!